*"The Prayer of Jabez* is terrific. Jabez's cry was that God would bless him so that he could bless others, change his generation, and change the world."

JASON PERRY, *PLUSONE*,
2001 DOVE AWARD WINNER,
NEW ARTIST OF THE YEAR

"I was just blown away by the simple truth in the prayer of Jabez. It's challenging, and it really has touched my life."

JEFF DEYO,
*SONIC FLOOD*

"Not since *Experiencing God* have I read a devotional so potentially life changing! I'm not much of a reader, but I became absorbed with this book and have immediately experienced the *awesome* rewards of praying the prayer of Jabez. Thank you, Dr. Wilkinson, for revealing to me, in a new way, the power of prayer!"

SCOTT ROBERTS,
*SOLOMON'S WISH*

"Since hearing about Jabez, I walk around with a different composure, in a different mood. His experience has taught me to live expectantly, to be aware that God is at work around me and in me. Instead of being self-centered, I'm looking around to see—*What has God prepared for my life today?* Who does He want me to meet, to bless? I live differently than I did."

GEOFF MOORE, CONTEMPORARY
CHRISTIAN RECORDING ARTIST

"This book really challenged me to put aside all my selfish little worries and realize that we are praying for Him to help us do what He needs us to do. It's okay to ask for God's blessing because through it we're going to be able to reach more people."

RACHAEL LAMPA,
DOVE AWARD WINNER

"This is a *great* model for prayer and a great encouragement to pray! I have seen God move because I've expected Him to move and *asked* Him to move. It all points to God."

ELI, CONTEMPORARY
CHRISTIAN RECORDING ARTIST

# the Prayer of Jabez for Teens

the **b**reakthrough **s**eries

# the Prayer of Jabez for Teens

## Bruce Wilkinson

**with David Kopp**

Multnomah® Publishers *Sisters, Oregon*

THE PRAYER OF JABEZ FOR TEENS
published by Multnomah Publishers, Inc.
© 2001 by Bruce Wilkinson

International Standard Book Number: 1-57673-815-9
Cover design by David Carlson Design

Scripture quotations are from:
*The Holy Bible,* New King James Version
© 1984 by Thomas Nelson, Inc.

Also quoted: *The Living Bible* (TLB) © 1971. Used by permission of
Tyndale House Publishers, Inc. All rights reserved.

*The Holy Bible,* New International Version (NIV) © 1973, 1984 by
International Bible Society, used by permission of Zondervan Publishing House

*Multnomah* is a trademark of Multnomah Publishers, Inc.,
and is registered in the U.S. Patent and Trademark Office.
The colophon is a trademark of Multnomah Publishers, Inc.

Printed in the United States of America

For information:
MULTNOMAH PUBLISHERS, INC. • P.O. Box 1720 • SISTERS, OREGON 97759

01 02 03 04 05 06 07 08 — 10 9 8 7 6 5 4 3 2 1 0

To our daughter, Jessica.
Every year, you get more amazing!
And fourteen is no exception.
You are such a special gift to our family.
Love, Dad

Special thanks to my writing partner,
David Kopp,
for your help getting this message into words;
Heather Harpham Kopp,
for your skillful editing;
Marcus Brotherton,
for your excellent contributions;
and to the many teens who
contributed stories,
for showing me what God is doing right now
in answer to bold prayers.

AND JABEZ CALLED ON THE GOD OF ISRAEL SAYING OH THAT YOU WOULD BLESS ME INDEED AND ENLARGE MY TERRITORY THAT YOUR HAND WOULD BE WITH ME AND THAT YOU WOULD KEEP ME FROM EVIL THAT I MAY NOT CAUSE PAIN. SO GOD GRANTED HIM WHAT HE REQUESTED.

# TABLE OF CONTENTS

PREFACE 13

CHAPTER ONE: LITTLE MAN, BIG PRAYER 15

CHAPTER TWO: SO WHY NOT ASK? 31

CHAPTER THREE: BORN FOR MORE 45

CHAPTER FOUR: THE POWER SOURCE 63

CHAPTER FIVE: GLADIATOR LESSONS 79

CHAPTER SIX: MAKING JABEZ YOURS 95

STUDY GUIDE:
JABEZ CONVERSATIONS 107

Dear Teenager:

I wrote the *The Prayer of Jabez for Teens* with you in mind. Young people around the world are leading the way in a prayer revolution. They're seeing God do miracles. And I don't want you to miss out on what's happening.

This little book starts with everything we put in the original, bestselling *The Prayer of Jabez;* then we ask the question:

If God wanted to change the world with a teenager like you, how would He want you to pray?

From there, I show you how to pray a daring prayer that can shape each day of the rest of your life. It's short—only one sentence with four parts— and found in a part of the Bible most people don't often read. But I believe it contains the key to the most exciting and significant life you could imagine.

Want to find out more about the Jabez revolution?

I hope you do!

*Bruce H. Wilkinson*

# CHAPTER 1

# little man, big prayer

Sometimes life seems to unwind like an enormous brown ball of string. Every morning you roll out of bed, pick up the string where you dropped it the night before—and off you go. Today seems pretty much the same as yesterday. One more day, one more length of string—and that big brown ball just keeps unwinding....

But some days aren't like that at all. They don't unwind like string; they land like a brick. One thing happens, and everything changes.

It could be...

- a phone call,
- a move to a new town,

- something someone says or does,
- a decision,
- an accident.

Whatever it is, that one thing changes your life, maybe for the better, maybe not. It's like you turned a corner and walked smack into a world you've never seen before.

This book is about one thing—a little prayer that will change your life.

Sometimes I think of this prayer as an invisible revolution because it starts so deep inside you. You change what you know; then you change how you think and feel; then you change what you ask God for and what you expect. It all feels so mysterious and out of sight...but then one day—zap! You look around ("Hey, did a brick just land around here?") and you realize your life has changed...and it's a whole lot better!

If you've ever thought that your life should be about more than just unwinding another day's worth of brown string, you're ready to meet a man named

Jabez (I pronounce that JAY-bez, but you can say it any way you like).

When Jabez was still trying to decide what kind of life he wanted, he looked at who he was. He didn't like what he saw. He looked at what he had to work with and who his family was and what tomorrow might bring, and *he didn't like any of it.* He felt like a nobody with no future. He probably could have described himself right then with words like *boring, loser,* or just plain *stupid.*

But he didn't.

Instead, he did one thing. He prayed a simple prayer.

I want to tell you more about this man named Jabez and his prayer, but first I want to ask you something. *Are you ready to do one thing today that could change your life from ordinary to extraordinary?*

If so, keep reading. *The Prayer of Jabez for Teens* is going to show you what happens when young people decide to reach for an amazing life.

As it turns out, that's exactly the kind of life God promises. Let me show you what I mean....

## Asking for a Big Life

When I was five, I wanted to drive a fire truck. When I was seven, I wanted to be a cowboy. When I was ten, I wanted to play for the New York Yankees, or maybe be a mafia hit man. (Is this starting to sound familiar?) When I was fifteen, I wanted to be an Olympic high jumper.

But when I was twenty-six and about to finish college and grad school, I didn't have a clue what I wanted to be. Except for one thing—I wanted my life to count for God.

I remember those days very well. I remember feeling a little uncertain and a lot in the dark. Darlene, my wife, and I often prayed together about what would come next. What did God want for our lives?

One day I heard a speaker named Dr. Richard Seume ask this question: "Do you want a bigger vision for your life?"

*Bigger?* I asked myself. *Well, maybe, but I'm already planning to serve God and live a good life. Isn't that big enough?*

Dr. Seume based his challenge on the shortest life

story I had ever heard—only three sentences in the Old Testament. The biography in question belonged to a man named Jabez. The first thing the Bible says about Jabez is that he was "more honorable than his brothers" (1 Chronicles 4:9). Dr. Seume said that's what we should want for our lives, too. Jabez wanted to be more and do more for God.

> ## Prayer is an invisible revolution.
> It all feels so mysterious and out of sight... then one day—zap!

I went home, stood in my kitchen, and stared out the window. *Lord,* I prayed, *I think I want a life like that. I want to be more honorable for You.* But questions kept tugging at my mind. *What exactly did Jabez do to rise above the rest? And why did God answer his prayer?*

I picked up my Bible and read verse 10—the prayer of Jabez. Something in his prayer would explain the mystery. It just had to. Think about it: Here was a guy who got into the history books because of what he prayed and what happened next. Standing in my kitchen, I read his prayer over and over, searching with all my heart for the future God might have for someone as ordinary as me.

The next morning I prayed Jabez's prayer word for word.

And the next.

And the next.

Do you know what? Thirty years later, I haven't stopped praying the prayer of Jabez, and God hasn't stopped answering. If you were to ask me what sentence—other than my prayer for salvation—has changed my life the most, I would tell you that it was the prayer of a little-known man named Jabez.

## Jabez and You

I think you have an appointment with God on this page just like I did in that kitchen. Why do I think that? Because you're reading this book right now. God brought you here because He knows your hopes

JABEZ CALLED
TH

and dreams. He knows that you don't have it all together in your personal life yet. But He knows, too, that you want something better for your life than just the usual ho-hum—for that matter, better than just the usual "success" you see on the street or on TV.

In a lot of ways, you're like Jabez. You're at the beginning of your life, but already you know that there are a hundred ways to get stuck, to get it wrong, to mess things up permanently. And you don't want that. You want something bigger. Maybe even something huge.

You're just not sure how to get from here to there.

But you're about to find out. As you learn about Jabez and his little prayer, you're going to meet a God who can make it happen in your life. You may not have met this God before. He is:

- a God who wants to give you more than you've ever thought to ask for.
- a God who has a big and important plan for your life.

- a God who is in the business—every day—of doing miracles through people just like you.

Do you want that? Or do big promises sound suspicious to you?

Listen! I know the message of this book is true because God has proved it in my own life. And because He's proving it in thousands of lives right now around the world. And, most of all, because it's in the Bible.

## The Man with No Future

Someone once said that there is really very little difference between people—but that little difference makes a great deal of difference. Jabez isn't a big star in the Bible like Noah or Moses or David. In fact, most people have never heard of him. (He's like that kid at school who isn't very talkative or popular. A lot of people don't even realize he exists.)

Are you ready

To make matters worse, Jabez's story is tucked away in 1 Chronicles, one of the least-read sections of one of the least-read books of the Bible. The first nine chapters of 1 Chronicles are a long list of unusual names that even brilliant scholars have a hard time pronouncing.

Take chapter 4: "The sons of Judah were Perez, Hezron, Carmi, Hur, and Shobal." And that's just the beginning.

*Ahumai...*

*Ishma...*

*Idbash...*

*Hazelelponi...*

*Anub...*

I'll forgive you if you have a sudden urge to put this book down and reach for the TV remote. But stay with me. Because forty-four names into the chapter, our story breaks through:

to do one thing today that could **change your life** from ordinary to extraordinary?

Now Jabez was more honorable than his brothers, and his mother called his name Jabez, saying, "Because I bore him in pain." And Jabez called on the God of Israel saying, "Oh, that You would bless me indeed, and enlarge my territory, that Your hand would be with me, and that You would keep me from evil, that I may not cause pain!" So God granted him what he requested. (1 Chronicles 4:9–10, NJKV)

That's it. In the next verse, the roll call picks up as if nothing has happened—*Chelub, Shuah, Mehir*...

Do you see what just happened? Something about Jabez made the historian stop mid-drone, clear his throat, and switch tactics. "Ah, wait a minute!" he seems to say. "You just *gotta* know something about this guy named Jabez. He stands head and shoulders above the rest!"

What was it about Jabez that made him so special? You can search from front to back in your Bible, as I have, and you won't find any more information than we have in these two verses. The even-shorter version of this already short story would look like this:

- Things started badly for a person no one had ever heard of.
- He prayed an unusual, one-sentence prayer.
- Things ended amazingly well because God granted his request.

Clearly, the outcome can be traced to his prayer. Something about Jabez's request changed his life and left a permanent mark on the history books of Israel. I'll restate his four requests again:

1. "Please bless me indeed!"
2. "Please enlarge my territory!"
3. "Please put Your hand on me!"
4. "Please keep me from evil!"

At first glance, the four requests might strike you as sincere or smart but not terribly remarkable.

Yet just under the surface of each lies an amazing and powerful truth that many Christians *never* understand.

When you put this prayer to work in your life, things will start to happen.

## Jump into the River!

When was the last time God worked through you in such a way that you knew beyond a doubt that He had done it? In fact, when was the last time you saw miracles happen on a regular basis in *your* life? If you're like most teenagers I've met, you wouldn't know how to ask for that kind of experience—or even if you should.

Recently, I was in Dallas to teach on the Jabez blessing to an audience of nine thousand. Later, over lunch, a man said to me, "Bruce, I heard you preach the message of Jabez fifteen years ago, and I haven't stopped praying it. God's miraculous answers have been so overwhelming that I have just never stopped."

Teenagers around the world are learning to pray in the same way. In fact, I know students who have used the prayer of Jabez all through junior high and high school. I know youth groups that have prayed it for the days leading up to a mission trip.

Just the other day, I received an e-mail from a kid named Brandon. "When you pray like Jabez, get ready for things to happen!" he wrote. He told me that he'd had one of the worst days he could remember recently—his car got a flat tire and his girlfriend

God knows that you want **something better** for your life than just the usual ho-hum.

dumped him. But he decided to keep praying the little prayer we're talking about. By the end of that week he had led three friends to accept Jesus as their personal Savior. And listen to this—they all *came to him* asking to talk about God! "God answers prayers," Brandon wrote. "I'm only sixteen and God is using me in ways I never thought I could be used."

God really does have an extraordinary life waiting for you. He's been planning all the great things you will do for Him since before you were even born! (Ephesians 2:10). All you have to do is want His best for your life…and ask for it with all your heart.

Think of it this way: Instead of standing near the river's edge, begging for a cup of water to get you through each day, you'll do something unthinkable. You'll take the little prayer with the giant prize and *jump into the river!* At that moment, you will begin to let the currents of God's grace and power carry you along. God's great plan for you will surround you and sweep you forward into the exciting life He has waiting.

If that is what you want, say good-bye to all those days that unwind like a boring brown ball of string. And keep reading.

**Think what a million teenagers could do…**

# THE GOD of ISRAEL

## CALLED ON JABEZ

OH THAT YOU WOULD BLESS ME INDEED

## so why not ask?

Can you remember begging your parents for things when you were really little? It was so easy. Candy, ice cream, toys, a new basketball, the latest doll that burps and wets and comes with thirty-seven outfits. Maybe you put your latest wish on your birthday list, then campaigned every day to get what you wanted just in case your parents didn't realize how serious you were....

Looking back, you were pretty selfish, right?

Sure.

But then again, maybe not.

Look at it this way: You were convinced that your mom and dad loved you and *wanted* to make you happy. You knew they were rich (when you're little, all grown-ups are rich). You knew that if they gave you what you wanted, it didn't mean someone else wouldn't get something good from their parents—I mean, no one would be *losing* because you were *getting*. And finally, you knew that if you really, really wanted something, your dad and mom would want to be the first to know about it. Caring comes naturally to them. That's their job.

So what was selfish about asking? You see, when you were a child, it made all the sense in the world to ask for whatever you wanted, as often as you wanted it.

Now, let me ask you a question. *Is it possible that God wants you to come to Him with the same happy (okay, slightly crazy) confidence of a child and ask Him to give you the very best He has for you?*

I've met so many Christians who think that such an idea is wrong. They assume that they'll seem greedy or immature if they ask God for too many blessings. But that's not what Jabez believed. Somewhere in his bones he knew something that most of us miss. He was convinced that God loved him and wanted to *really* bless him and that He could because He had unlimited power and resources. That kind of trust in his heavenly Father made it natural for Jabez to pray exactly the kind of request God wants to hear.

Maybe it wasn't just faith that made him pray like that. Maybe he wanted to try an experiment. Or maybe he had run out of alternatives.

Where do you see yourself in his story?

Let's take a closer look.

## Trading Pain for Gain

As far as we can tell, Jabez lived in southern Israel during the time of the judges (about 1200 B.C.). He was born into the tribe of Judah, the same tribe that David and Jesus came from later. Jabez eventually had many descendants, which would explain why his name appears in the lists of names in Chronicles.

Yet his story really begins with his name: "His mother called his name Jabez, saying, 'Because I bore him in pain.'" In Hebrew, the word *Jabez* means "pain."

What was his mother thinking when she gave him such a terrible name? Did she have a difficult childbirth? Did she not want another baby? Was her new baby boy really *that* ugly? We just don't know. I've heard of guys named Peter Rabbit or Forrest Bush (his sister's name was Rose). But Pain beats them all. Something pushed Jabez's mother into picking an extremely unfortunate name.

> **What** was his mother thinking when she gave him such a **terrible name?**

Whatever the reason, Jabez grew up with a nan any boy would love to hate. You can bet he went through childhood getting teased and bullied.

Yet the heaviest burden of Jabez's name was how it defined his future. In Bible times, a name was often taken as a prediction. For example, *Solomon* means "peace," and sure enough, he became the first king of Israel to reign without going to war. A name like Pain did not hold much hope for a good life.

Now think about this: In Jewish culture, a boy entered manhood at age thirteen. Soon after, he started making plans for his future—what he was going to be and do, who he was going to marry. Chances are good, then, that when Jabez finally faced the facts and decided to pray, he was still a teenager.

At that moment, a breakthrough happened. He quit thinking about his name. He stopped being angry with his mom. He turned away from the teasing. He gave up worrying about his past and his "fate."

And he prayed. He didn't just sort-of pray, either. When he prayed, he started off with the biggest, most outrageous prayer he could imagine...

"Oh, that You would bless me indeed."

Can you feel the intense desire behind his request? In Hebrew (the language 1 Chronicles was written in), adding *indeed* is like adding five exclamation points, or writing a request in capital letters and underlining it. That's how Jabez prayed that day.

If I could make a movie to capture the meaning of this moment, I would show young Jabez standing before a barrier as big as the Great Wall of China. Sunk into the stone is a huge iron door that's sealed shut. Jabez is staring at it. He knows there's no way over it and no way around.

But raising his hands to heaven, the young man cries out, "Father, oh, Father! Please bless me! And what I really mean is…bless me a lot!"

With the last word still echoing against the wall, Jabez hears a tremendous crack. Then a groan. Then a rumble as the huge gate swings away from him in a wide arc. There, stretching to the horizon, are fields of blessings.

And Jabez steps forward into a completely different life.

## Blessing Is Not About Sneezing

Before you can pray like that, you need a clear understanding of what the word *blessing* means. Seems like we hear *bless* or *blessing* every time we go to church. We ask God to bless our parents, our day at school, and the peas we're about to eat. It's something your teacher says when she hears you sneeze.

No wonder the meaning of blessing gets watered down to something like "Have a nice day." No wonder so many Christians aren't as desperate as Jabez was to receive it!

To bless in the biblical sense means to ask for supernatural favor. When we ask for God's blessing, we're not asking for more of what we could get for ourselves. We're sincerely asking for the kind of good things that only God has the power to know about or give. That's why the Bible says, "The Lord's blessing is our greatest wealth. All our work adds nothing to it!" (Proverbs 10:22, TLB).

And let me tell you something else about blessings—a blessing from God is something you can *feel*. When God gives you the desires of your heart, He might give you "stuff," but He's always reaching for *your heart*.

Imagine that you are an empty drinking glass

sitting on the end of a dock on a beautiful lake. The sun comes up. You're hot and thirsty. "Man! I could drink this whole lake!" you exclaim. Then God comes along and fills you to the brim with cold, refreshing water. Now you're satisfied. You don't need or want one more drop.

That's what a blessing from God feels like.

God always **blesses** for a purpose.

If you think about it, this explains why some poor people you know are the happiest people you've ever met—their glass if full. And why some very wealthy people you meet have lots of stuff but are still unsatisfied.

I've noticed something else: Truly blessed people go around blessing others. God always blesses for a purpose. He wants His goodness to bless you, then flow through you to others. Praying for God's blessing doesn't mean asking for more stuff just so we can spend it on ourselves. It means asking for God's favor so we can serve Him better and be a blessing to others.

Do you want God's blessings and want them *indeed?* They are waiting to be yours.

But there's a catch.

## You Have to Ask

What if you found out that God had it in mind to send you twenty-three specific blessings today, but you got only one? What do you suppose the reason would be?

There's a story about a Mr. Jones who dies and goes to heaven. St. Peter is waiting at the gates to give him a tour. Heaven is quite an amazing place, but in the middle of all the stunning sights, Jones notices a weird looking building—sort of an enormous warehouse. When he asks Peter to see inside, Peter hesitates. "Ah, you really don't want to look in there," he tells the new arrival.

But Jones can't stand not knowing a secret. *What could be waiting for me in there?* he wonders. So he argues until his tour guide gives in.

When Peter opens the door, Mr. Jones almost knocks him over in his hurry to get in. What he sees is row after row of shelves, floor to ceiling, each stacked neatly with white boxes tied with red ribbons.

"These boxes all have names on them," Jones mutters aloud. Then turning to Peter he asks, "Do I have one?"

"Oh, sure," Peter says. Then he tries to get Jones to leave. But Jones won't be stopped. He dashes toward the *J* aisle. There are only 640 billion Joneses in heaven, so it doesn't take him long to find his box. Peter catches up with him just as he is slipping the red ribbon off his box and popping the lid. Looking inside, Jones has a moment of instant recognition. Then he lets out a deep sigh like the ones Peter has heard so many times before.

Because there in Mr. Jones's white box are all the blessings that God wanted to give to him while he was on earth, but Mr. Jones never asked.

Don't miss the big idea in this story!

"You do not have because you do not ask," the Bible says (James 4:2). "Ask," promised Jesus, "and it will be given to you.... What man is there among you who, if his son asks for bread, will give him a stone?... If you then, being evil, know how to give good gifts to your children, *how much more will your Father who is in heaven give good things to those who ask Him!"* (Matthew 7:7, 9, 11, emphasis mine).

You see, even though there is no limit to God's goodness, if you didn't ask Him for a blessing yesterday, you didn't get all that He wanted to give you.

That's the catch—if you don't ask for His blessing, you forfeit those that will come to you only by asking. God's blessings in our lives are limited only by us, not by His resources, power, or willingness to give.

If you doubt that God could be that giving, maybe you need to meet the real God....

## God's Nature Is to Bless

Maybe when you pray you're still talking to a stingy, storybook God you made up when you were little. Maybe the God in your head is a clone of a mean, angry person in your life. Maybe you've never really asked God to introduce Himself to you.

Moses did. He asked God, "Please, show me Your

glory" (Exodus 33:18), and God answered. Listen to how God described Himself: "[I am] the LORD, the LORD God, merciful and gracious, longsuffering, and abounding in goodness and truth" (Exodus 34:6). This is God's self-portrait, and it's incredible, isn't it? He is the most wonderful person to be around in the entire universe. If you took all the best qualities in all your friends and multiplied them by a thousand, you would just be getting started on having a friend like God!

Jabez had grown up hearing about this God of Moses—the God who had freed Israel from slavery in Egypt, brought them safely through the Red Sea, and given them the Promised Land. If God could do all that, surely He could make something out of one boy's ordinary life.

Because Jabez knew the truth about who his God was, he didn't tell God what to give him. He let

God decide what his blessings would be. In the same way, we can confidently ask God to bless us and leave the details up to Him.

God wants to bless you and me because *it is in His nature to bless.* That's why you need to make a life-long commitment to ask God every day to bless you—and while He's at it, bless you *a lot!*

Maybe you think your name could be just another word for pain or trouble. Friend, the prayer of Jabez is for you. Jabez—Mr. Pain himself—changed his life because he refused to let any obstacle, person, or opinion loom larger than God's true personality.

And God's personality is to give—and give again—to someone just like you!

With a simple prayer, you can escape your past. You can change what happens, starting now.

The Jabez Million.

They're up to something big.

OH THAT YOU WOULD ENLARGE MY TERRITORY

# born
## for more

I was so desperate to get money for dates that I took a job at a chicken prison. It was my first paying job, and I really wanted to make it work. But as you can imagine, the prison—okay, it was an egg farm—was a terrible place. You could smell it from a mile away. The huge metal sheds were full of hanging wire cages. Each cage was crammed with dozens of upset chickens with nothing to do but eat and peck at each other and squawk at the top of their lungs and lay eggs. My job was to collect eggs as fast as possible and keep the cages closed.

The minute I walked into that place, I knew my life was on the line. Those hens didn't like me stealing their eggs. After only five minutes, I dropped one. Two thousand beady eyes let me know that if there was ever a jailbreak, I was chicken feed.

After an hour of scooping and stacking, I discovered that I was allergic to feathers. When I wasn't scooping, I was blowing my nose. When I wasn't blowing, I was sneezing and juggling eggs.

Minutes turned into hours. I couldn't believe my life had come to this—chickens squawking, feathers flying, eggs rolling, and me sneezing.

Have you had a moment like that when you looked at your life and thought, *Is this what my life has come to? Is this all it's going to be?*

Jabez must have had a moment like that. Since his family members were farmers or herdsmen, he'd had plenty of time doing chores to wonder, *Is this*

Is this what my life has come to? Is this all it's going to be?

*going to be the whole story of my life?*

The answer was easy. *Yes—unless I get some help!*

That's when he decided to ask for more. In the second part of his prayer, he pleaded, "Oh, that you would enlarge my territory!"

## "I Was Born for More than This!"

Depending on which Bible translation you're reading, *territory* might be translated *coast* or *borders*. For Jabez, this word meant as much as the words *homestead* or *frontier* meant to the American pioneers. It described a place of one's own with plenty of room to grow.

So when Jabez prayed for a larger territory, he was asking God for a raise, a promotion, a bigger and better life...all rolled into one. Why? Because Jabez knew that the size of his territory exactly

equaled the size of his opportunity. And the little patch of ground he could see now just wasn't enough. He wanted more. In fact, he felt deep in his heart that he was born for more.

And he was right. He lived at a time in the history of Israel when the Jews were still taking over the Promised Land. God had told them to take *all* of the land. Yet, seven times in one chapter (Judges 1), we read that tribes of Israel failed to win—or even try to win—all the land that God had promised to give them.

Can you imagine how disappointed God must have been in His people's small dreams? Do you see why Jabez's prayer was exactly the kind of prayer God was waiting to hear?

Just as it is highly unusual to hear anyone pray, "God, please *bless me!*" so it is rare to hear anyone plead, "God, please *give me more territory!*" Why? Maybe because we think our lives are too full already. Or it's easier to settle for what we already

OH THAT YOU WOULD

have, even if we don't like it. Some of us even settle for collecting eggs.

But God wants us to want to receive everything that He wants to give us and do through us. After all, His reputation and His good plans for the world are at stake!

Jabez was born for more. His story proves it.

I was born for more. My story proves it. I didn't even make it till the lunch break. My boss watched me sneezing and trying to hang on to eggs; then he broke the news. My career as an egg collector was over. I lost my first job the same day I started it!

*You* were born for more, too. And right now, God is waiting to prove it. The Bible says, "Eye has not seen, nor ear heard, nor have entered into the heart of man the things which God has prepared for those who love Him" (1 Corinthians 2:9).

So the next good question is, "What could 'more' look like in my life?"

ENLARGE MY TERRITO

## The Land That Borders Yours

In the same way that God blesses you *for a purpose,* He wants to enlarge your territory *for a purpose.*

My favorite word for "taking territory" is *ministry.* But don't let that word scare you. Ministry is just a big word for what happens when God uses you to reach someone. When it happens, you know it. And it's the most exciting and meaningful experience on the planet.

Does that mean you have to stop everything and become a preacher? Probably not.

I know stockbrokers who pray that God will increase the value of their investments in such a way that their clients will *know* that God did it. I know stepmoms and teachers, warehouse workers and pro football players, who pray every day to take more territory for God.

God usually expands your territory first by increasing the personal influence *you already have.* He'll use you to minister to those people whose "land" borders yours—family, neighbors, friends, kids you meet at school, people you know at church or at your job.

You see, everybody has territory. And God wants to increase and enlarge yours, no matter what your age or abilities.

"Dr. Wilkinson, you have no idea how shy I am," Sara wrote recently. "But let me tell you what's happening on my campus since I began to ask God for a larger life. A girl named Kirsten cornered me about

My favorite word for "taking territory" is ministry. But don't let that word scare you.

a month ago and just seemed to want to talk. I asked God to help me, and mostly I just listened. Since then this girl has been the cause of three other kids asking to talk to me. Two have become Christians. And I think Kirsten's going to be next!"

Whatever your circumstances, your prayer for a larger life—with more influence and more results—might sound something like this:

*O God, I want to do great things for You! Please, Lord, expand my opportunities and increase my influence because I want to touch more lives for You.*

## "Hello, I'm Your Jabez Appointment"

When you begin to pray for more ministry, you'll start having surprising encounters. You'll feel like God looked at your day and at someone else's, then found where your paths could cross, and said, "Hmm, I think I'll have them meet each other...*here!*"

I call these Jabez Appointments. Sometimes these encounters will be with people you already know. But sometimes a person you don't know will show up on your doorstep or in the seat next to you...and you'll *know* that God put them there.

"The last day of spring break I woke up in the morning and prayed for a Jabez kind of day," writes Bess. "Actually, I prayed specifically that God would use me to be a witness on the plane back home. Well, on the plane I was sitting next to a man who noticed a book I was reading called *Reasons to Believe.*"

That started a conversation. The man asked Bess

what the book was about. "I did my best to explain without sounding ridiculous," says Bess. After she explained that the book presented the author's research about Jesus, the man said he'd like to read the book, too. On the spot, she gave him her copy and he began reading. "I've been praying for him ever since!" Bess says.

Bess had her Jabez Appointment.

One afternoon Darlene heard a knock on our front door. She'd been asking God to help her reach out to the neighborhood. When Darlene opened the door, a woman was standing there in tears. "Ma'am," she said, "I don't really know you, but my husband is dying and I have no one to talk to. Can you help me?"

Darlene had a Jabez Appointment.

OH THAT YOU WOULD ENLARGE MY TERRITORY

I've had Jabez Appointments in airports, on elevators, at football games. They seem to follow a predictable pattern:

1. Ask God to enlarge your border today. Ask Him to show you your appointment.
2. Keep your eyes peeled and your heart open (God is full of surprises!).
3. When you think a person might be your appointment, ask that person, "How can I help you?" They might be surprised at first, but usually they'll show you exactly how you can help.
4. While you're talking to the person, keep asking God to work through you. Remember, this is God's work. You don't have to make something happen. You don't have to be someone you're not.
5. Afterward, write down what happened so you can remember and learn from it.
6. Thank God for enlarging your borders—and keep praying!

You can trust that God will never send someone your way that you can't help. God will always show you what to do and will help you do it.

With that in mind, are you ready to ask God for something huge, something outrageous...like maybe a tropical island?

I know some college students who did just that.

## Asking for Trinidad and a DC-10

While speaking some years ago at a large Christian college in California, I challenged students to pray the Jabez prayer for more blessing and greater influence. I told the two-thousand-member student body that they should set a big ministry goal, something worthy of a college their size.

"Why not look at the globe and pick an island," I suggested. "When you have picked it out, put together a team of students, charter an airliner, and then take over the island for God."

Some students laughed. Some thought I was nuts. But nearly everyone listened. So I kept talking.

Recently, I had been to the island of Trinidad just off the coast of South America. I described some of the needs I saw there. "You should ask God for Trinidad," I said, "and a DC-10."

I had no immediate takers.

Still, my radical proposal got a lot of students thinking. Most students told me they wanted to use their time and talents for God, but they didn't know where to start. They listed everything they *didn't* have—skill, money, courage, and so on.

Some students laughed.
Some thought I was nuts.

I spent most of that week asking a question: *God loves you infinitely and wants you in His presence every moment, and if He knows that heaven is a much better place for you, why has He left you here on earth?* Most students weren't really sure. They'd never thought about that before. With each one, I gave what I think is a biblical answer to the question: *Because God wants you to be moving out your boundary lines, taking in new territory for Him. Maybe even an island…*

God was at work. A week after I returned home, I got a letter from a student named Warren. He told me that he and his friend Dave had decided to ask God to bless them and enlarge their borders. More specifically, they had asked God to give them the opportunity to witness to the governor of the state *that very weekend.* Throwing their sleeping bags in Warren's '63 Plymouth Valiant, they had driven the four hundred miles to the capitol to pound on doors.

The letter continued:

By Sunday night when we got back from Sacramento, this is what had happened:

We had expressed our faith to two gas station attendants, four security guards, the head of the U.S. National Guard, the director of the Department of Health, Education, and Welfare for the state of California, the head of the California Highway Patrol, the governor's secretary, and finally the governor himself.

As God is making us grow, we are thankful and scared stiff. Thanks again for your challenge!

That was just the beginning. Over the next weeks and months, a vision for more territory swept the campus. By fall, a student team headed by Warren and Dave had mounted a major mission project for the following summer. They called it Operation Jabez. Their objective: assemble a team of student workers, charter a jet, and—you guessed it—fly to the island of Trinidad for a summer of ministry.

And that is exactly what they did. One hundred and twenty-six students and faculty signed up. By the time the jet took off fully loaded from Los Angeles, Operation Jabez had trained teams ready to minister through drama, construction, sports clinics, vacation Bible school, music, and home visitation. The college president called Operation Jabez the most important student ministry venture in the school's history.

OH THAT YOU WOULD ENLARGE

Two students asked God to enlarge their territory—and He did! One little prayer changed boundary lines. One little prayer touched the lives of thousands of people.

## Your Front-Row Seat

To pray for larger borders is to ask for a miracle—it's that simple.

But do you believe miracles still happen? Many Christians I've met do not. Often, this is because they confuse miracles with magic. I remind them that miracles don't have to break the laws of nature to be a supernatural event. When Christ stilled the storm, He didn't set aside the laws of nature—the storm would eventually have subsided on its own. Instead, He directed the weather pattern. When Elijah prayed for it to stop raining, God didn't make clouds suddenly vanish. Instead, He worked through the natural cycle of drought and rain.

God is ready to do miracles in your life. Just make sure you're looking for the real God, not a "magical"

or cartoon God. A cartoon God might turn a short, white kid from Manitoba into Michael Jordan. Or make that painful divorce and remarriage in your parent's lives suddenly disappear—*poof!* Or get you an A in algebra when you haven't even gone to class.

But the real God does miracles of a different kind. He'll…

- arrange your day so that you connect with just the right person,
- give you words to say when you can't think of any,
- give you wisdom that you didn't know you had,
- bring you the money you need,
- make you strong when you feel weak,
- change you on the inside,
- work through you even though you're still just you,
- love you always, always…even when you feel like a disgusting glob of gunk on someone's shoe.

The most exhilarating miracles in my life have always started with a bold request to expand God's kingdom *a lot*. When you take little steps, you don't need God. But when you jump into the rushing river of God's plans and ask Him for more ministry, God goes to work all around you.

When He does, you have a front-row seat in a life of miracles. It's more exciting than you could ever dream. But as you're about to discover, it can get a little scary, too...

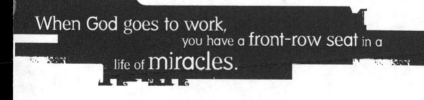

When God goes to work, you have a front-row seat in a life of miracles.

OH THAT YOUR HAND WOULD BE WITH ME

# the power
## source

When you ask God to expand your borders, He'll expand them up to the edge of your comfort zone…and then *He'll keep right on going.*

He'll open up possibilities you've never thought of before. He'll ask you to do things you've never done before (and that you're pretty sure you can't do). It will feel like He takes you to the edge of a cliff and says, "Let's go for a walk."

That's when you'll meet the giant of fear. You'll want to run. Turn back. Say it was all just a mistake…

Just ask Ben. He told me that God had answered his prayers for more territory by giving him leadership positions at school and in his community. He said his life had changed completely from the year before. But now he had a new problem.

"Since God expanded my horizon, I have begun to wonder if I have what it takes to do this. Sometimes, I feel overwhelmed and afraid." He wanted to know what to do.

Another person wrote, "I'm beginning to feel the fear part of the Jabez prayer. Once the blessings flow, once the territory is expanded—then what? Yikes!"

If you haven't run into the giant of fear yet, you will soon. But here's what I tell kids who get this far: "Friend, you are right on track! In fact, you're just getting to the good stuff!"

Why? Right here—when you feel that you've gone past what you can do—is where the miracles begin. Right here is where you will start to see God work in your life in ways you've only read about in books or heard about from missionaries.

And once you do, you'll *never* want to turn back.

## Can't Shake That Feeling

I remember what happened the first time I asked God to expand my borders *a lot*. Darlene and I had

started a little Bible study ministry in our basement.
It began to grow. And grow. Soon I was being asked
to speak. To manage a staff. To publish a magazine.
To run a business…

One morning I woke up and knew for certain
that I was in way too deep. I couldn't shake the feeling that God had made a mistake. After all, I was
only trained to be a Bible teacher.

I couldn't shake the feeling that God had made a mistake.

I decided to seek the counsel of a trusted Bible
teacher named John Mitchell. He was in his eighties
by then, but he had been a spiritual father to thousands. I described to Dr. Mitchell what I thought God
was calling me to do. Then I told him that I had discovered I couldn't do it.

"Son," he said, "it's about time! That feeling you
have now is called dependence on God. Actually, if
you lose that feeling for too long, you're in danger

of becoming self-sufficient. That's when you stop living by faith. That's when the miracles will stop!"

I was shocked. I had come to him for help to get rid of those feelings. "You're saying, Dr. Mitchell, that the feeling that I just can't do it is the feeling I'm *supposed* to have?"

"Why, certainly, young man!" he said, beaming. "That's the one all right."

It's exciting and a little frightening, isn't it? As God's blessed sons and daughters, we are expected to attempt something big enough for God that failure is guaranteed…unless God steps in.

That explains why taking new territory for God:

- pushes you into trying something new,
- requires more courage, ability, time, or money that you thought you had,
- sets you up to risk looking like a fool and a loser, and
- seems impossible.

I'll admit, movie heroes think dependence is a bad idea. But you and I were made for it. Dependence upon God makes heroes of ordinary people like Jabez and you and me. How? We're forced to pray the third part of Jabez's amazing little prayer:

"Oh, that Your hand would be with me!"

Jabez didn't begin his prayer by asking for God's hand to be with him. When we step out for God, we think we have things under control. But once our boundary lines stretch and grow, we need power—and fast!

That's why you could call God's hand on you "the touch of greatness." You do not become great; you become dependent on the strong hand of God. Your huge need gives God a huge opportunity to do something exciting. And He becomes great through you.

## A Ladder to the Clouds

One day when our children were preschoolers, Darlene and I took them to a large city park in southern California. It was the kind of place that makes a grown-up want to be a kid again. The park had swings, monkey bars, seesaws, and slides. There wasn't just one slide, but three—small, medium, and giant. David, who was five, took off like a shot for the small slide.

"Why don't you go down with him?" my wife suggested.

I had another idea. "Hang on," I said. "Let's wait and see what happens." So we relaxed on a nearby bench and watched. David climbed to the top of his slide, waved, and whizzed down. No problem.

He moved to the medium-sized slide. He had climbed halfway up the ladder when he turned and looked at me. But I pretended not to notice. David thought for a moment, then carefully backed down the ladder one step at a time.

"Honey," my wife said, "you ought to go help him out."

"Not yet," I replied, hoping my smile would let her know I wasn't just being careless.

David spent a few minutes watching other kids climb up, shoot down, and run around to do it again.

Finally his mind was made up. He climbed all the way up…and slid down. Three times, in fact, without even looking at us.

Then we watched him turn and head toward the giant slide. Now Darlene was getting worried. "Bruce, I don't think he should do that by himself. Do you?"

It was the kind of place that makes a grown-up want to be a kid again.

"No," I replied as calmly as possible. "But I don't think he will. Let's see what he does."

When David reached the bottom of the giant slide, he turned and called out, "Dad!" But I glanced away again, pretending I didn't hear.

He peered up the ladder. To a little boy, that monster slide must have looked like it reached to the clouds. He watched an older boy go flying down the slide. Then, against all odds, he decided to try. Step-by-step, hand over hand, he inched up the ladder. But he hadn't gone up a third of the way when he froze. By this time, an older boy was coming up behind him and yelled at him to get going. But David couldn't. He couldn't go up or down. He had reached the point of certain failure.

I rushed over. "Are you okay, son?" I asked from the bottom of the ladder.

He looked down at me, shaking and hanging on for dear life. And I could tell he had a question ready.

"Dad, will you come down the slide with me?" he asked. The older boy was losing patience, but I didn't want to miss this moment.

"Why?" I asked, peering up at him.

"I can't do it without you, Dad," he said, trembling. "It's too big for me!"

I stretched as high as I could to reach him and lifted him into my arms. Then we climbed that long ladder up to the clouds together. At the top, I put my son between my legs and wrapped my arms around him. We started laughing. Then we went zipping down the slide together, laughing all the way.

That is what God's hand is like.

You try something that's too big for you. You could fail—or you could pray. So you pray, "Father, please do this in me because I can't do it alone! It's too big for me!" Then you step out in faith to do and say things that could happen only with His power.

Afterward, you shout, "God did that, nobody else! God carried me, gave me the words, gave me the power—and it's awesome!"

## His Hand, His Spirit

The *hand of the Lord* is a biblical term for God's power and presence in the lives of His people (see Joshua 4:24 and Isaiah 59:1). In the book of Acts, the rapid spread of Christianity was explained by one thing: "The hand of the Lord was with them, and a great number believed and turned to the Lord" (Acts 11:21). The "hand of the Lord" is another way of talking about the power of the Holy Spirit.

Early Christians spent a lot of time praying together, waiting on God, and asking for His power (see Acts 2:42–47 and 4:23–31). Why? They had just had their borders expanded *to the whole world*. Jesus had told them, "Go into all the world and preach the gospel" (Mark 16:15). Talk about reaching the point of certain failure! The disciples' job was clearly impossible.

Yet when the Holy Spirit filled them, these ordinary men had the confidence to witness to everyone (Acts 1:8). When others saw it happening, they knew that God was at work. The Bible says, "Now when they saw the boldness of Peter and John, and perceived that they were uneducated and untrained men, they marveled. And they realized that they had been with Jesus" (Acts 4:13).

When was the last time you pleaded with God, "Lord, please put Your hand upon me! Fill me with Your Spirit!"? When was the last time your youth group did that?

Once you have that power, you are ready to succeed at something big and overwhelming—something where everyone will know that *only* God could have done it.

I want you to meet some kids who decided one summer to put God's reputation on the line...and see what He would do.

## Twelve Teens and a Bag of Tricks

When I was a youth pastor at a growing church in New Jersey, twelve high school kids proved to me that the hand of God is available to every believer who asks. Here's what happened:

After praying most of the school year about a summer ministry project, we decided to do six weeks of youth evangelism in the suburbs of Long Island, New York. How many kids total would we reach for Christ? We didn't know—we just knew it would be a lot!

We decided on a three-part strategy. We would begin with backyard Bible studies, switch to beach evangelism in the afternoon, and then wrap it up with an evening outreach in different churches. Sounds simple, but let me tell you, the team—youth pastor included—felt overwhelmed by the task.

We invited a specialist in children's ministry on Long Island to give our youth group some training. He told us that getting as many as thirteen or fourteen kids in a backyard club would be a smashing success. But while he was talking, I felt God was calling us to pray for a specific number of changed hearts—a number that would prove that only He could have done it.

After he left, I told the group, "If we don't have one hundred kids in each club by the end of the week, we should consider it a failure." Suddenly, all of us wanted to get down on our knees and pray!

I'll never forget those wonderful prayers. "Lord, please bless us!" and "Lord, I know it's way over my head, but please, give me a hundred kids!" and "Lord, by Your Spirit, pull off something great for Your glory!"

Parents kept telling our team that our plan was impossible. And I'm sure they were right. But it started happening anyway. The first week, four of the six teams had more than a hundred children crammed into their meetings. By the end of the week we had shared the Good News with more than five hundred kids.

Then the beach phase of our mission to Long Island kicked in. I bought a beginner's magic kit—you know, "everything you need to amaze and impress your friends." Then I stayed up until 3 A.M. learning

how to make an egg "disappear." By the next afternoon, we were unrolling our free show in the sand and
pleading with God for His hand to be upon us.

We decided to ask the Lord for thirty decisions
for salvation—by the end of the first day.

You are right where **God wants you...**
*a prayer away from*
**a miracle.**

Our audience grew from a single row of squirm-
ing children to more than 150 onlookers. We rotated
the entertainment from magic shows to storytelling
to gospel presentations. Soon, adults began edging
closer. Finally clusters of teenagers started joining the
crowd. By the end of the afternoon we had reached
a count of 250. And when we finally gave an invita-
tion, thirty people accepted Jesus Christ as their
Savior—right there on the beach.

Once we had established our beach ministry, we
added an evening program for youth in local

churches. God blessed our efforts beyond anyone's expectation—but right in line with the size of our Jabez prayer. By the end of our six-week outreach, we counted up 1,200 new believers on Long Island.

Do you know what else happened? Twelve high school kids came back to their New Jersey neighborhoods convinced that *God can do anything.* And it wasn't too long before the whole congregation was touched by revival.

Impossible? Not at all. All because twelve students asked for blessings indeed, for more territory for God's glory, and for His hand of power to be upon them.

Jesus said, "The things which are impossible with men are possible with God" (Luke 18:27).

## Right Where God Wants You

Have you noticed that no matter how many sermons we've heard about God's power to work through us, we keep missing that little word *through?*

Sure, we say we want God to work *through* us, but what we really mean is *by* or *in association with.* What we're really thinking is *Lord, let me do this by my power and abilities, and You just add your blessing to it.* Yet God's work can be done only by God's power. That's why, when the Jews returned from captivity, God told them, "Not by might nor by power but by My Spirit, says the LORD of hosts" (Zechariah 4:6).

So when you face your moment of certain failure, when you look down and think you're about to fall, when you feel like yelling "YIKES!" at the top of your lungs, ask God to put His hand upon you.

You are right where God wants you…a step away from a whole new way of living, a prayer away from a miracle.

You could
be one of
The Jabez Million.

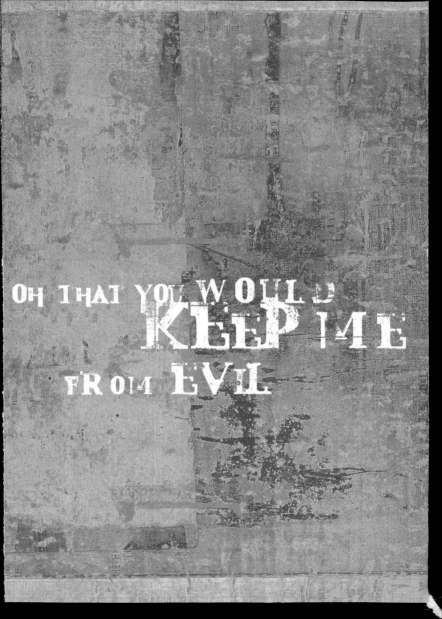

OH THAT YOU WOULD KEEP ME FROM EVIL

# gladiator lessons

I have a drawing that shows a Roman gladiator with a very big problem.

Somehow, the gladiator has dropped his sword, and he has turned to flee for his life. A hungry lion--claws out, jaws open—is leaping through the air after him. The crowd in the arena has jumped to its feet, watching in horror. They *know* what's going to happen next!

The caption under the drawing reads:

*Sometimes you can afford to come in second.*
*Sometimes you can't.*

The drawing reminds me how important it is to come in first against temptation. In this contest, there's no second place. The drawing also reminds me of Jabez's unusual plan for winning.

After getting supernatural blessings, influence, and power, Jabez might have figured he could win a fight against any lion. But the fourth part of his prayer shows that he understood things differently. He knew that he had a dangerous enemy and that he needed help.

So he prayed, "Oh, that You would keep me from evil!"

In the previous chapter, you prayed for supernatural power to work through your weakness. In this chapter, you'll learn how to ask for supernatural help to protect you from Satan's desire to eat you for lunch. I'm going to show you how this part of the prayer works for Jabez warriors like you and me. It's practical. It's easy to understand. And—with God's help—it's pure genius!

## From Blessings to Battles

You might be wondering why we're talking about temptation and evil in a book about blessing. But think about this: Once you start moving into new territory for God, guess whose territory you're invading?

That's right—Satan's.

I'm not trying to scare you. Because Jesus died for our sins and rose from the dead, Satan is already a defeated enemy. The Bible says, "He who is in you is greater than he who is in the world" (1 John 4:4).

But Satan is still actively working against God's plans for the world and for you. The more Jabez successes you have, the more you're going to become familiar with the enemy's unwelcome jabs—distractions, temptations, opposition. You'll realize, "Hey, there's a force out there that hates God, and he doesn't like what I'm doing, either!"

But Satan isn't the only problem. Our desires for the wrong things and our sinful nature can get us in trouble without any help from the devil! (see James 1:14).

That's why the final request in Jabez's prayer is so important.

The truth is, if you feel that temptations *don't* bother you anymore, you should probably worry!

Let me illustrate. When I was a student in seminary, I overheard a conversation I'll never forget. I was standing in line behind another student. He was talking to Dr. Howard Hendricks, a professor of mine. The student was excitedly telling Dr. Hendricks how well everything was going.

"When I first came here," the student said, "I was so tempted and tested that I could barely keep my head above water. But now—praise God!—my life has smoothed out. I'm hardly being tempted at all!" I remember thinking, *Wow, I'd give anything if my life was like that!*

But instead of looking pleased, the professor looked deeply alarmed—not the reaction the student was expecting. "That's about the worst thing I could have heard," Dr. Hendricks told the surprised student. "What you just told me shows that you're no longer in the

Blessings **always** come with battles.

battle! Satan isn't worried about you anymore."

When we follow Christ, blessings always come with battles. That's why praying to be kept from evil is so necessary if you want to keep experiencing a truly blessed life.

## Air Warfare over Chicago

I think you'll discover, as I have, that the times when you need this prayer the most are when you're feeling tired or under stress. For you, this might come at the end of finals week, when you're feeling under pressure at home, or after you've stayed up late with friends. For me, it often comes after I've been involved in demanding ministry over the course of many days.

Years ago, a cab picked me up in downtown Chicago and was whisking me toward the airport. I slumped in the backseat, glad to be heading home. I had been the featured speaker for a week at a Bible college in the city. God had moved in remarkable ways. I counseled a lot of students, too—seventy-six, to be exact (I kept a log). But now I was exhausted. Staring out at the traffic, I reached for the Jabez prayer.

*O Lord,* I pleaded, *I have no resistance left. I'm completely worn out in Your service. I can't cope with temptation. Please, keep evil far from me today.*

When I boarded the plane, I found I'd been assigned a middle seat. I hate middle seats! And things got worse. The man on my left pulled out a pornographic magazine.

I looked the other way and groaned. *Lord,* I prayed, *I thought we had a deal here!* But before the plane even lifted off, the man on my right pulled out his own skin magazine.

I closed my eyes. *Lord,* I prayed, *I can't cope with this today. Please save me from temptation and chase evil far away!*

The plane rose into the sky above Chicago. Suddenly the man on my right swore, folded up his magazine, and put it away. I looked at him to see what had made him change his mind. Nothing, as far as I could tell. Then the man on the left swore too and closed up his magazine. Again, I couldn't find any reason for his decision. God had answered my prayer!

We were over Indiana when I began laughing out loud. They both asked me what was so funny.

"Guys," I said, "you wouldn't believe me if I told you!"

## Praying "Keep Away"

Think for a minute about how you pray when you face temptations. Do you mostly ask just for strength to not give in? There's nothing wrong with that prayer, but it's not the way Jabez prayed.

He didn't pray "Keep me *through* evil" but "Keep me *from* evil."

You see, Jabez understood what that doomed gladiator didn't: Our most important strategy for defeating the roaring lion is to *stay out of the arena.* Jabez didn't ask for more lessons in sword fighting or courage to fight lions.

He asked to be kept away from evil altogether.

Jesus taught us to pray that way, too. When Jesus taught his friends what we call the Lord's Prayer, He said, "When you pray, say…. Do not lead us into

OH THAT YOU WOULD KEEP ME FROM EVIL

temptation, but deliver us from the evil one" (Luke 11:2, 4).

Look at that prayer again. There's nothing about asking for special powers, just "Please, keep me away from temptation!"

When was the last time you prayed like that? In the same way that God *wants* you to ask for more blessing, more territory, and more power, He *wants* you to ask to be kept away from evil. I promise that when you begin to focus less on beating temptation and more on avoiding it, you'll make a huge spiritual leap forward!

Relying on your human "weapons" can turn you into cat food.

Being tempted isn't the same thing as sinning—that's another of Satan's deceptions. Let's say you're tempted by sexual sin. Or tempted to gossip. Or tempted to take something you really want that isn't yours. If you hang around these temptations thinking you can beat them, you're already making the wrong choice. You're not on neutral ground. You're in

the arena, and a raging lion is ready to pounce. That's
why the Bible tells us to run away from temptation
(2 Timothy 2:22).

Do you still think you're a world-class lion tamer?
Let me show you how relying on your human
"weapons" can turn you into cat food:

- *Your common sense can get you in trouble.* Look at
  what happened to Adam and Eve in the Garden
  of Eden. They knew just enough to think they
  knew it all, and Satan tricked them into disobey-
  ing God.
- *Your previous experience can get you in trouble.* Just
  because you beat temptation once doesn't mean
  you'll be safe the next time. The deepest grief I've
  seen in Christian young people is among those
  who have experienced extraordinary blessings,
  territory, and power...only to slip into serious sin.
  The Bible says, "Take heed lest you fall."
- *Your feelings can get you in trouble.* Most of us figure
  this out early on, but we still don't really believe
  it. We still try to muddle through. "Follow your

heart," the world says. "Do what you feel is right." But your desires and needs and lusts can convince you something's right when it's really all wrong.

Jabez warriors beat temptation by avoiding it. They pray every day that God will keep them far from evil. These prayers for deliverance are the prayers of God's real champions. And He loves to answer them.

## Ashley's SPAM Attack

My story about the pornographic magazines shows how God does His part to keep us from temptation when we ask Him to. The next story shows you how you can do your part to stay away from temptation. After all, there's no point in praying not to be tempted if you keep going to Temptation Playground.

Let me ask you, what would happen if you made hard choices to cooperate with God and turn off unnecessary temptations that flood over your life every day? Okay, you can't live in a vacuum tube,

OH THAT YOU WOULD

and God doesn't want you to. But what if you got rid of some of the obvious trash—even for a few days?

Ashley, a teen from Detroit, wanted to find out. She decided to take the SPAM challenge. No, this story isn't about canned meat. SPAM stands for Spiritual Preparation And Meditation. The challenge was to fast for a week to two months from secular books, TV, magazines, movies, and music. The purpose of fasting (or doing without for a chosen length of time) was to prepare her to hear God more clearly.

You're probably already thinking, "That sounds like torture!" So did Ashley, at least at first. Here's her story:

> An entire week without my favorite shows, favorite groups, and fashion mags? Yeah, right. The thought seemed unbearable to me. But after a few days of God tugging at my heart, I knew I should give it a try. And I could probably use the break from all the worldly junk I've let trickle into my life.

KEEP ME FROM EVIL

So I began "spam-ing." I put away all my secular CDs—bye-bye boy bands, hello Point of Grace and Steven Curtis Chapman. I gave the TV remote a rest and bought some Christian novels to help pass the time. I also bought a journal to write both my thoughts and the things God would teach me during SPAM week. I was ready to take my relationship with Jesus Christ to a new level.

The first day was easy. In fact, I enjoyed it. God revealed some interesting things to me as I read my Bible. Stuff that I hadn't seen before, or perhaps had deliberately overlooked. I thought to myself, *This isn't so hard.*

I was wrong. The next day as I watched the numbers of the clock change, I knew my favorite show was about to begin and I was stuck doing SPAM. I regretted ever making that commitment. But I resisted the urge to turn on the TV and instead grabbed my journal. I began writing down my thoughts. Eventually I reached for my Bible. Wow! It was like a light turned on! That was a major breakthrough for me.

It still wasn't easy. At times I really had to fight the urge to buy a certain CD, or I had to put a magazine back on the rack. But I stuck with the plan because I wanted to concentrate on whatever is true, noble, right, pure, lovely, and admirable (Philippians 4:8).

The remaining days flew by, and I was sad to see the week come to an end. Some of my friends asked me how the week went. My answer is that staying away from all those influences helped me to see things differently. Stuff that I used to think was okay to listen to, watch, or read now looked wrong to me. I felt different, and because of that I wanted to act differently.

God used those short seven days to change my life. That time ignited my faith and opened my eyes to other friends who need a spiritual boost. It's not always easy, fun, or convenient. But when you make the effort to stay away from the junk, you can hear God's voice and grow in Him.

Ashley (spam I am)

I think Jabez would have liked the SPAM plan. He wanted to live free from bondage to sin. "Stay out of the arena of temptation whenever possible," he would tell you. "Never live in fear or defeat. By God's power, you can stay clean, stay safe, and stay on course for God's amazing best for your future!"

## Sin Is a Thief and a Thug

Which brings me to my last point. *Only sin can cut you off from the blessing and power of God.* You see, Satan doesn't tempt you just to put a black mark on your chart. He wants you to fall into sin so he can steal your blessings and stop the miracles that God is doing in your life.

Ultimately, he wants you to sin because sin hurts you.

That's why Jabez ends his last request with these words: "that I may not cause pain." Some Bibles translate it, "so that I will be free from pain," or something like that. The reason for the difference is that the Hebrew just says, "pain not." So you can see why translators could write it both ways. And both ways are completely true.

But don't miss the big idea: *Sin causes pain.* In fact, the Bible says, "The wages of sin is death" (Romans 6:23). Just look around at the Christian pastors and youth leaders who fall into sin. After starting out strong, they decide that the lion of temptation is nothing but an overgrown house cat. Then one day they drop their sword. Next thing you know they're caught in the jaws of sin, they drop out of ministry, and they hurt a lot of people.

Jabez knew that giving in to temptation would cause harm, both to himself and to others. And he begged God to keep it from happening.

You need to do the same. Ask God to keep evil away from you. And do your part to cooperate by keeping yourself as far away from temptations as possible. Then you will be on your way to a permanent place on God's honor roll.

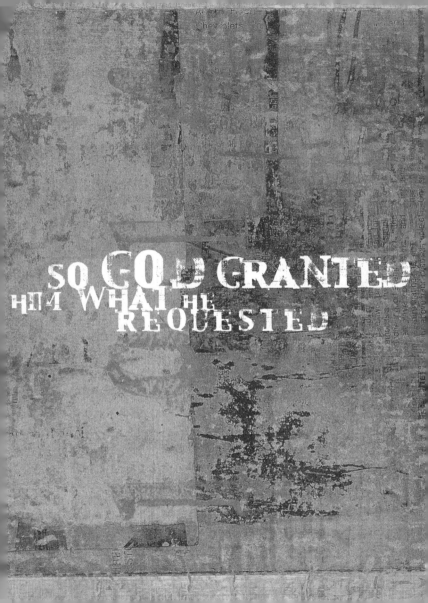

SO GOD GRANTED
HIM WHAT HE
REQUESTED

# making jabez
## yours

At the start of this book, I asked you a question: *Are you ready to do one thing that could change the rest of your life?*

I wanted you to see that God has a much larger, more important, and more exciting life waiting for you than you ever imagined.

So, let me put it to you again: Are you ready to do one thing that could change the rest of your life?

If your answer is yes, I have a simple plan for you. It looks pretty ordinary, but don't be fooled. It's part of the Jabez revolution, and it's helping to change the lives of millions around the world.

## "My Name Is Jabez…"

For the next thirty days, make the prayer of Jabez belong to you. Tell yourself, "My name is Jabez, and this is my prayer." Then pray it into your life. Here's my simple plan to make praying Jabez really stick and become part of your daily routine:

1. Every morning, pray the Jabez prayer.
2. Mark off a calendar every day to show how well you keep your promise.
3. Write out the Jabez prayer and tape it somewhere where you won't miss it.
4. Reread *The Prayer of Jabez for Teens* once every week for four weeks. Ask God to show you the important stuff you might have missed.
5. Tell one other person about your thirty-day plan. Ask him or her to check up on you.
6. Keep a journal of your Jabez adventures. Describe your Jabez Appointments. Write down what you're learning.
7. Start praying the Jabez prayer for your family, friends, church, youth group, and school.

If you put this simple plan to work, you will develop a permanent habit of reaching for God's best.

Of course, reading about this plan and actually doing it are two very different things. You can tape the Jabez prayer on every wall in your house and nothing will happen. You can talk about it, believe it, know it, recommend it…. Nothing will happen. Nada. Zip.

Tell yourself, "My name is Jabez, and this is my prayer." Then pray it into your life.

But when you do one thing—*pray it*—you take that first step in the right direction, then another and another, and change happens. God will release His power in your life.

## The Rest of the Story

In the first chapter of this book, I told you how I stood in my kitchen and decided to make the prayer of

Jabez a regular part of my spiritual life. Let me tell you the rest of the story.

Over the years, my wife and I have never stopped praying Jabez because *God has never stopped answering!* First, the teaching ministry called Walk Thru the Bible got too big for our basement. It grew from twenty-five conferences each year to more than fifty *each weekend.* It grew from publishing one magazine to ten—recently we published our 100-millionth copy!

Our borders have grown so much that not long ago we asked a question: "Lord, what are *Your* borders? What do You want done?"

Obviously, His borders are big enough to take in the whole world. So that is what we've been praying for. *O God, let us reach the whole world for You.*

In January 1998, we began WorldTeach, an exciting ministry to Bible teachers in every nation on earth to teach the Bible to their own people. The fifteen-year goal is to find and train 120,000 believers who would teach a new Bible course each year.

God is answering our Jabez-sized projects faster

than anyone ever imagined. In 2000, we opened a new WorldTeach nation every seventeen days (we're up to thirty-eight countries now), and as of May 2001, our total number of teachers has risen to nearly nine thousand—three thousand teachers ahead of schedule.

As *The Prayer of Jabez for Teens* is preparing to go to press, I'm in Indonesia, helping to launch WorldTeach in southeast Asia. In this Moslem nation, God has allowed us to train over one thousand WorldTeachers in six major cities.

What God is accomplishing can't be explained in human terms, and no one can take any credit for it. I just want you to see what happens when ordinary people pray big prayers…and step forward to see what God will do!

## Running to Win

Do you think God honors some of His children more than others? I do. He honored Jabez for wanting with all his heart what God wanted for him.

God is waiting to honor young people like you who desire to reach for a "more honorable" life. (Like one teen told me, "I've always known I was a light just waiting to shine.") When you stand before Him in heaven someday, you don't want to hear God say, "You did okay." You want to hear Him say, "Well done!"

To say that you want to be more honorable in God's eyes is not pride or self-centeredness. More honorable is what God said about Jabez, not what Jabez said about himself. So when you desire to be on God's honor roll, you are pleasing God.

Because you have JESUS, you have more spiritual resources than Jabez did.

I've noticed that winning honor nearly always means leaving ordinary, mediocre, and average behind. But it doesn't mean we suddenly become supersaints. In God's opinion, more honorable people are ordinary folks who are pursuing a bigger life for Jesus with all their hearts.

"One thing I do," wrote Paul, "forgetting those things which are behind and reaching forward to those things which are ahead, I press toward the goal for the prize of the upward call of God in Christ Jesus" (Philippians 3:13–14).

## The Jesus Advantage

As you continue to pray the Jabez prayer, never forget the Jesus Advantage. What do I mean by that? Think about it. When Jabez was alive and prayed his prayer, Jesus hadn't yet come to earth to die for our sins. So, while Jabez was ahead of his time and blessed because of his prayer, he didn't have the spiritual benefits that come from knowing Jesus.

But you do. And because you have Jesus, you have more spiritual resources than Jabez did to help you become more honorable. That's the Jesus Advantage.

When Jabez prayed for God to bless him, he couldn't receive the greatest blessing of all, which is believing in Christ and obtaining eternal salvation. *But you can*: "He who believes in the Son has everlasting life" (John 3:36).

When Jabez prayed for God to expand his territory, he couldn't call on the power of the Holy Spirit to help him. *But you can*: "He [Jesus] said to them…. 'You shall receive power when the Holy Spirit has come upon you; and you shall be witnesses to Me'"(Acts 1:7–8).

When Jabez prayed for God's hand upon him, he couldn't experience the grace and power of Jesus in his weakness. *But you can*: Paul wrote, "He [Jesus] said to me, 'My grace is sufficient for you, for my power is made perfect in weakness.' Therefore I will boast all the more gladly about my weaknesses, so that Christ's power may rest on me" (2 Corinthians 12:9, NIV).

When Jabez prayed to be kept from evil, he couldn't call upon on the One who was tempted like us but never sinned. *But you can*: "For in that He [Jesus] Himself has suffered, being tempted, He is able to aid those who are tempted" (Hebrews 2:18).

By far the best place to meet God is by getting close to the person of Jesus Christ. God's purpose in sending His Son, Jesus, to earth was demonstrate His desire to bless us with salvation and eternal life. If you haven't met God personally through Jesus Christ and accepted His death for your sins, please don't wait a minute longer. You're missing out on the biggest, most important blessing in the universe!

## Hold on Tight

I told you that only one thing is necessary to live the Jabez life. But Mark from Oklahoma thinks it ought to be two. He wrote:

> All I can say is two things. Number one, *The Prayer of Jabez* should come with a warning label. An earnest and sincere prayer of Jabez to our Father results in miracles! You're right. Miracles are the everyday occurrences in the life of a Christian who diligently prays this little prayer. Hold on tight!
>
> Number two, *The Prayer of Jabez* should also come with seat belts! It is a wild ride! Since I have prayed Jabez, a number of athe-ists have taken a very sudden interest in my

Christian messages on various Web sites. I have atheists e-mailing me, calling me, working with me, even bumping into me in the middle of the night in a faraway town. I've never talked about Jesus with more atheists in my entire life!

I am not sure why I'm getting these advanced witnessing jobs from my Father, but I trust that He knows what He's doing in His perfect plan laid out for my life!

If you're ready to join the Jabez revolution, strap yourself in for a wild and wonderful ride. God's about to release His awesome power in your life. And for all eternity, He will lavish on you His honor and delight.

If you're ready to join the Jabez revolution, strap yourself in for a wild and wonderful ride.

## Are you one of **The Jabez Million?**

You're invited to put your mark on the world today by joining the Jabez prayer revolution right now. One million teenagers are banding together to pray the Jabez prayer for ourselves and our world every day for a year.

**Our objective? Enormous.**

[ *to reach the world for God* ]

**Our odds? Ridiculous.**

[ *without God, that is* ]

**Our prayer? Outrageous.**

[ *but God is waiting to hear and answer* ]

Visit the Web site below and tell us you want to be counted. We'll tell you what happens next.

The Jabez Million is 1,000,000 teens around the world asking God for the world...every day.

God has been waiting for you to ask—and ask with all your heart—for what He wants most to give. It's time to ask...

**The Jabez Million**
Visit us at

**www.prayerofjabez.com/teens**

# jabez conversations

Use the resources on these pages as thought starters for your personal study or for group use. If you are a leader and want to create a learning experience for your youth group, be sure to visit www.prayerofjabez.com/teens for our posting of *The Prayer of Jabez for Teens, Leader's Guide.*

## Chapter One: Little Man, Big Prayer

*Big Ideas.*

No matter who you are or what your circumstances, God has an important and fulfilling life waiting for you. When you put His goodness, love, and power to the test by asking for His favor, He will use you for His purposes in the world. You will become one of His "more honorable" heroes in history.

*Conversation starters.*

1. What one decision has changed your life the most so far?

2. Describe a life that you think would really count for God. Do you think God wants to give you that life?

3. In what ways are your life and Jabez's life alike? In what ways are they different?

4. Do you feel like you're ready to reach for a "more honorable" life? Can you think of anything that's stopping you?

5. Have you ever felt God working through you and around you in a powerful way? What did it feel like? What happened?

## Chapter Two: So Why Not Ask?

*Big ideas.*

God wants to bless you because He loves you, and besides, He's a giving God! Whether they're big or little, God's blessings are something you can experience—they fill you up inside. God blesses you for a bigger purpose, too—so you can be a blessing to others. It just doesn't get any better than "the blessed life." But there's a catch. You have to ask God for it.

*Conversation starters.*

1.  What's the biggest blessing you've had in your life that you knew was from God?

2.  What person has blessed your life the most? Why?

3.  If you could ask God for anything in your life, what would it be? Would you feel selfish asking for it? Do you think God would think you're being selfish to ask for it?

4.  Have you usually thought of God as stingy and judgmental or generous and gracious?

5.  Have you ever sensed that God gave you something or did something for you so you could bless someone else with it? If so, what happened?

## Chapter Three: Born for More

*Big Ideas.*

God wants us to expand our influence and impact for Him (He knows that's where we find the most satisfaction and excitement in life anyway!). He wants us to be more and do more for Him. How much more? Well, God loves *the whole world* (does that give you any ideas?). One word for *territory* is *ministry*. Ministry is what happens when we let God use us in someone else's life. We start expanding our influence for God with those who are close to us (everyone has territory). But God can bring us together with people we've never met. You could call these encounters Jabez Appointments—divinely arranged meetings where God gives you new territory for a big and exciting purpose. Get ready to watch a miracle unfold, right before your eyes.

*Conversation starters.*

1.  What's the biggest dream you've ever had for a career or ministry for your life?

2. What person in your life, who is not a parent or sibling, inspires you the most to be more and do more for God? What is it about their example that makes such an impression on you?

3. Have you usually thought that you could have an important and influential life? Or have you usually thought you'd never have that kind of life, or if you did, that you'd have to wait a long time for it? Why?

4. Have you ever had what you think was a Jabez Appointment—a surprising encounter with another person that seemed to be arranged by God? What happened?

5. How would your life change if you thought that God wanted you to expand your ministry—and look for Jabez Appointments—*every day?*

## Chapter 4: The Power Source

*Big Ideas.*

As soon as you step out to do something big for God, you realize you can't do it alone. You need God's power—a lot of it, and fast! In fact, you might feel afraid and overwhelmed. But those feelings probably mean you're right on track. After all, you can't do God's work without God's power. So ask to be filled with the Holy Spirit. When you ask, God gives you His Spirit so He can work *through* you to reach the world. He wants to use you in surprising, important, and exciting ways, starting now.

*Conversation starters.*

1.  Can you think of a time or event in your life where you were certain that God's power made something happen? What happened?

2.  Do you know a person who seems to understand how to depend on God's power to succeed? How does this ability seem to affect their lives?

3.  Name three things you're good at. How might

God want you to use those talents in ways that are so big or scary you'd have to rely on Him?

4. Why do you suppose God likes to put us in a place where we feel like we're in over our heads?

5. Next time you feel like you're in too deep for God, what could you do besides turn back? How might your life change if you didn't turn back?

## Chapter Five: Gladiator Lessons

*Big Ideas.*

When you take territory *for* God, you're taking it *from* Satan. That means you can count on facing temptation and opposition. But instead of praying just for safety or strength, ask God to keep you away from evil. Jesus taught the disciples to pray in the same way—"Lead us not into temptation, but deliver us from evil." When you ask Him, God will answer. He'll keep you away from temptation. Just be sure to do your part to keep temptations out of your life. Then you'll be spared the pain that sin always brings.

*Conversation starters.*

1. Would you describe yourself as a person who "plays around with temptation" or as a person who "works hard to avoid temptation"?

2. What person comes to mind when you think of someone who sets an inspiring example for how to live well and stay away from temptation?

3. What particular temptations do you think you need to be most careful to ask God for protection from?

4. What pain have you experienced because of the sinful choices of others? What pain have you caused yourself and others because of sin in your own life?

5. Where do you think that playing with temptation or falling into sin may have stopped the flow of God's blessings in your life? What's one thing you could do to make a change?

## Chapter 6: Making Jabez Yours

*Big Ideas.*

You can make the prayer of Jabez the starting point for a lifelong habit of blessing and impact for God. A few simple steps will help you develop a permanent habit of reaching for God's best. God does honor some of His children more than others. The ones He honors want what He wants and run hard to win the prize of pleasing Him. As a Christian, you have the greatest gift of all—the Lord Jesus Christ—to bring you God's best, both for now and eternity.

*Conversations.*

1. Have your expectations of what's possible—and what God wants for you—changed since you started reading *The Prayer of Jabez for Teens*?

2. What might stop you from succeeding at the thirty-day plan to make the prayer of Jabez a lifelong habit? What could you do to avoid that problem, or succeed in spite of it?

3. What encouraging friends and wise mentors could you tell about your Jabez commitment? Describe one or two simple things they could do to help you succeed.

4. Have you asked Jesus to help you understand the blessing of your salvation and new life through Him? What do you think you might be missing?

5. If you wrote a three-sentence biography of all that you became and did for God in your lifetime, what would you want it to say?

# FREE—

## On-line:

### The Prayer of Jabez for Teens
### Bible Study with Leader's Guide

*The Prayer of Jabez for Teens Bible Study with Leader's Guide*
will be available on-line September 2001.

**Simply access:** www.prayerofjabez.com/teens

# The BreakThrough Series, Book One
## *The Prayer of Jabez*

*New York Times* # 1 Bestseller! 8,000,000 in Print

ISBN 1-57673-733-0

- The Prayer of Jabez Audio (available April 2001)
  ISBN 1-57673-842-6
- The Prayer of Jabez Leather Edition (available April 2001)
  ISBN 1-57673-857-4
- The Prayer of Jabez Journal (available May 2001)
  ISBN 1-57673-860-4
- The Prayer of Jabez Devotional (available May 2001)
  ISBN 1-57673-844-2
- The Prayer of Jabez Bible Study
  ISBN 1-57673-979-1
- The Prayer of Jabez Bible Study with Leader's Guide
  ISBN 1-57673-980-5
- The Prayer of Jabez Gift Edition (available August 2001)
  ISBN 1-57673-810-8

Visit www.thebreakthroughseries.com

# Next in The BreakThrough Series
# from Bruce Wilkinson

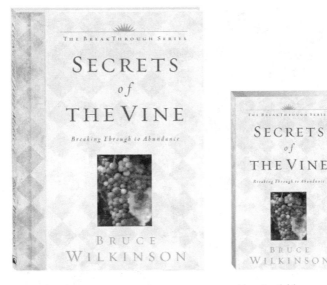

Secrets of the Vine

Dr. Bruce Wilkinson explores John 15 to show readers how to make maximum impact for God. Dr. Wilkinson demonstrates how Jesus is the vine of life, discusses four levels of "fruit bearing" (doing the good work of God), and reveals three life-changing truths that will lead readers to new joy and effectiveness in His kingdom.

ISBN 1-57673-975-9

Also Available on Audiocassette

Read by author Bruce Wilkinson

ISBN 1-57673-977-5

Lord, bless me indeed and enlarge my territory

Is **God** doing great things in your life? In your youth group? In your community? We want to hear from you!

Check out other real-life stories of the supernatural touch of God in the lives of teens—just like you!

# www.prayerofjabez.com/teens

Plus, some of your favorite recording artists talk about "The Prayer of Jabez"...**PlusOne, Stacie Orrico, Michael Tait, Rachael Lampa, Eli, Geoff Moore, Sonic Flood's Jeff Deyo, Kevin Max...**

We would love to hear from you.
Read amazing testimonies on the prayer of
Jabez or submit your own story.
Visit www.prayerofjabez.com
or Multnomah Publishers/Jabez Stories
P. O. Box 1720, Sisters, OR 97759